Stephen Cottrell is the Bishop of Reading. His many books include *I Thirst* (Zondervan 2003), the Archbishop of Canterbury's Lent Book for 2004; *From the Abundance of the Heart: Catholic evangelism for all Christians* (DLT 2006); *Do Nothing to Change your Life: Discovering what happens when you stop* (CHP 2007) and, most recently, *The Adventures of Naughty Nora* (BRF 2008), a collection of stories for children, and *The Things He Carried* (SPCK 2008). He is married to Rebecca and they have three boys.

The Things He Said

The story of the first Easter Day

STEPHEN COTTRELL

First published in Great Britain in 2009

Society for Promoting Christian Knowledge
36 Causton Street
London SW1P 4ST

British Library Cataloguing-in-Publication Data
A catalogue record for this book is available from the British Library

ISBN 978–0–281–06197–6

1 3 5 7 9 10 8 6 4 2

Designed and typeset by Kenneth Burnley, Wirral, Cheshire
Printed in Great Britain by Ashford Colour Press

Produced on paper from sustainable forests

For my parents

Lord, to whom can we go?
You have the words of eternal life.

(John 6.68)

Contents

Acknowledgements

From beginning to end, this book was written in Eastertide, most of it in Easter Week itself when I had a week off and stayed with my parents in Leigh-on-Sea. Each morning I set up the laptop at the table in their dining room and the book poured out. I returned there at the end of Eastertide for another couple of days to finish it. So first of all I want to thank them for their hospitality and support – not just with this book, but with everything.

In between the two chunks of writing I took these words that Jesus speaks on the first Easter Day as my text for pretty much every sermon I preached. I tried to inhabit the words and see where they led me. As Eastertide is the Confirmation season, I therefore want to thank the hundreds of people I confirmed in Eastertide 2009 and the thousands who heard these sermons. Their listening has helped shape this book.

Last but not least, Joanna Moriarty at SPCK has been a tremendous encourager, and at more than one extremely good lunch has cajoled this book into life.

Introduction

One of the great joys of episcopal ministry is the Eastertide rush of Confirmation services. This year I have baptized and confirmed hundreds of people. Most of my sermons have begun with the same question: what were the first words that the risen Christ said on the first Easter Day? And although I didn't actually put anyone on the spot – it is supposed to be a rhetorical question – quite a few people shouted out suggestions. In fact, after the first couple of sermons I urged people not to guess because they invariably got it wrong – and when this was the clergy it was slightly embarrassing. But the plain fact of the matter seems to be that people don't know. The story of the resurrection itself is familiar, but the words Jesus speaks have somehow evaded us.

Having, then, established that people don't know, I have wondered out loud what we think he might have said. Would it be something triumphant – 'I have risen from the dead!', or credal – 'I have conquered sin and death; I have opened the gate of glory'?

The actual answer is surprisingly different. So surprising, so apparently innocuous, that the words themselves have failed to stick in many people's minds. The most popular guess shouted out was 'Mary'. This is, of course, one of the things that Jesus says; but it is not the first.

So which is? Well, first of all it is something of a trick question. The answer is different in each of the four Gospels, and each Gospel has its own fascinating twist.

In Mark, Jesus does not say anything at all (or at least in the more ancient version of Mark that ends at 16.8). There is just silence and a disturbing presence. The women come to the tomb. They sense something has happened. They leave in fear.

In John's account – and the first part of this book sticks almost exclusively with John – Mary Magdalene finds the tomb empty, fetches Peter and John, but then when they leave she lingers at the tomb. She is the first person to actually see the risen Jesus (though she mistakes him for the gardener). He says to her, 'Why are you weeping?', and then, 'Who are you looking for?', and then simply her name, 'Mary'. She holds on to him and then Jesus says, 'Do not hold on to me, because I have not yet ascended to the Father. But go to my brothers and say to them, "I am ascending to my Father and your Father, to my God and your God"'. These are astonishing words: each one a book in itself. Jesus speaks to the sadness and then the lostness of Mary. He says her name. He points her beyond his presence with her in the garden to a new availability and a new relationship with God.

In Matthew, the women run from the tomb, having been told by the angels what has happened and what it means. They then meet Jesus who says to them, 'Greetings . . . do not be afraid: go and tell my brothers to go to Galilee; there they will see me.'

In Luke – and the second part of the book leans heavily on the Lucan narrative – there is no record of Jesus saying anything until the evening: then on the Emmaus road he comes alongside Cleopas and his companion and says to them, 'What are you discussing as you walk along?' They stop dead in their tracks (though they do not recognize him either) and say he must be the only person in Jerusalem who doesn't know what has been happening these past few days. 'What things?' says Jesus – and we tend to miss the humour here: after all, Jesus was the one person who did know what had been happening in Jerusalem that weekend! They then tell him all that we would now understand to be the gospel, but it is not good news for them. So Jesus says, 'Oh, how foolish you are, and how slow to believe all that the prophets declared. Was it not necessary that the Messiah should suffer these things and then enter into his glory?'

After this, Luke's and John's accounts combine: Jesus is known to Cleopas and his friend at the breaking of bread. They rush back to Jerusalem to tell the eleven what has happened. Jesus appears in their midst. 'Peace be with you,' he says. There is then a longer piece in Luke where Jesus instructs the disciples on the meaning of what has happened and on his ascension. He then tells them to wait in the city until they receive the power of the Spirit. John has Jesus saying, 'As the Father sent me, so I am sending you', and then breathes the Spirit into them there and then. For John, the gift of the Spirit is bound up with the Easter story itself. Luke establishes the more familiar liturgical pattern where, after the ascension, the disciples wait for the coming of the Spirit at Pentecost.

* * *

A popular Good Friday devotion is based upon Jesus' seven last words from the cross. Pieced together from the different Gospel accounts, the words are the stuff of Holy Week preaching. A good many clergy over many generations will have written sermons on them. Many books have been written about them. We experience these words as a way in to the deepest meaning of the Passion. But for some reason there has never been the same emphasis on the words that Jesus spoke on Easter Day: words, as it were, from an empty tomb. Because at first sight they seem casual, almost off-hand, they are passed over. They seem to pale against the drama of the event itself.

But these words deserve greater attention. The words from the empty tomb can speak to us as powerfully as the words from the cross. They can illuminate our understanding of the resurrection, helping us to penetrate its meaning and significance. They can also speak effectively of God's purpose for us today as we try to discover what it means to be an Easter people. The Christian faith stands or falls on the resurrection of Jesus – without it, says St Paul, we are to be most pitied – therefore it is these words that we must hear and respond to.

It is therefore striking and significant that many of the things Jesus says are questions: 'Why are you weeping?', 'Who are you looking for?', 'What are you discussing?', 'Was it not necessary . . . ?' Taken that the other common thread running through the resurrection stories is the fact that Jesus isn't recognized, these searching questions have the effect of confronting us with a risen Christ who cannot be easily pinned down ('Do not cling to me,' he says to Mary), who demands response. But it is not a coercive demand. It is more the magnetic attraction of great and puzzling beauty; the sort of beauty that takes us beyond ourselves. Just as great art poses great questions, so does the resurrection of Christ.

In this sense the resurrection asks as many questions as it answers. Therefore, in order to understand the resurrection we need (like the disciples on the Emmaus road) to have our eyes, and our minds, opened; open to the probing questions Jesus poses, open to his disturbing and surprising presence. What are the sorrows we are carrying and where do we expect to find comfort? Who (and what) are we looking for in life? What are the questions that concern us as we travel through life? And, crucially, who is Jesus Christ? Why did he suffer and die? What does this tell us about God? The whole Christian faith is a dialogue – an Emmaus road walk – and these questions are the agenda. But it is also about recognition. Being recognized by God (he speaks our name, and at every Confirmation I am reminded of this when I say to the candidates in turn, 'God knows you by name and makes you his own'); and responding: knowing Jesus as our Teacher and Lord. But the continuity and discontinuity between the Jesus of his earthly ministry and the Jesus of the resurrection mean that we discover him as the 'same person', the one who was killed on the cross; and a different person, the one who was raised with a new and incorruptible life. He therefore evades definition. Instead, he invites relationship. And it is in the relationships, through responding to his call and continuing the dialogue, that we begin to find out and dwell in the truth of his audacious claims: that his God is our God;

that we have a share in his risen life; and that we are commissioned to share his story with the world.

So the risen Jesus poses questions. But this is not a book of answers. It is a book designed to retell the story in such a way that we might slow down and hear it properly and therefore hear the questions clearly.

Stephen Cottrell

PART ONE

EARLY MORNING

Chapter 1

Nothing.

These are the never-ending years of being dead. The long, dark hours of the night turning slowly, vanquishing the light, the heavy blanket of the blackest hour shrouding the land, obliterating every detail.

Silence.

Not in this moment the silence of expectation, as when the pianist pauses before the completion of a well-known phrase and the heart leaps forward, knowing its end, longing for its conclusion; but the chill, ominous, dark reverberation of emptiness and lostness.

She lies in her bed and stares into the blackness. It is all ended. She is undone.

Then, in the fevered turnings of her imagination, she is, as it were, outside herself, standing before a well that is completely overgrown, suffocated with matted ivy and dense thorn. She knows she is dreaming, but at the same time she walks confidently into the dream. It is her only hope.

The night is as black as ever. The little moonlight that had led her thus far has expired. She is alone.

She stands at a place where she has stood many times before. She remembers these times. They were full of hope and optimism. The fresh, cool water she had raised from the depths of this well had revived and refreshed her, filled her with joy. But now it is defeated, barren and overgrown.

She falls to her knees. The wind has been taken out of the sails of her hoping. She dreams of water. She has to find out if there is any left. She stretches her hands forward on to the dry scrub of the ground. Hardly anything is growing around the well. The ground is dusty gravel, peppered with thistle and stone. She scrabbles in the darkness looking for a stone: looking for something to drop into the well, something to tell how far she has to go before the water rises again.

Her hand touches the polished smoothness of a perfectly round pebble. It seems out of place. It is something shaped by the operation of oceans, or the gentle caressing of a stream. But it is ready for this moment. Even as she picks it up there is a whisper of hope in her heart. But as her hand closes around it, she feels its icy coldness: cold like the night itself. There is hardly any warmth left in her body to change it.

She takes another step forward. She tears back the tangle of creepers and weeds that are almost burying the well, growing from the last remaining moisture that has clung to its crumbling walls. And then she lets the stone drop. The moment of release really is the last moment of hope.

And she waits. She imagines she can hear it turning in the air, but really there is nothing. It falls silently, hopelessly.

And she waits. She waits to hear the echo of the tiniest splash that will come back to her as blessing and comfort. But there is nothing.

How far will it fall? For how long will it go on falling? What depths will be plumbed? And when will there ever be an end to the agonizing hopelessness of hope forsaken?

'For he is dead, my beloved, the one in whom I hoped, the one who seemed to bring so much. And my hands are empty, and his tomb is full, and there is no sense to it any more.'

Falling and falling. Tumbling and tumbling. Darkness covering darkness, ever deeper into the heart of nothingness and emptiness and void.

She waits and waits. All through the hours of the night. All through the unending silence. But nothing. A silence that is worse than silence, not even the distant full stop of the thud of stone upon dry ground, but nothing, the grim foreboding of something emptier than emptiness. She lies on her bed, but she doesn't sleep. She just hears the stone falling and the silent emptiness of infinity enlarging and engulfing. She stares into the darkness. She can almost hear the milk curdling in the jug.

Deep calls to deep . . .

And the first sound to break the silence of the night? Her tears. Not the anguished howl that had ripped from her heart on that dreadful Friday afternoon – only two days ago – how could that be? How could days be so unendingly long, so empty? No, this was the almost immeasurable touch of a first raindrop on a spring leaf: her tear rolling from her eye, slowly traversing her cheek, leaving the faintest smudge of pain.

And then she sits bolt upright. Her hands grip the sides of her bed. The horrors of the night assault her: the sheer, bloody waste of it; the stupidity of dreaming and the un-avoidable inevitability of her own death. She didn't know when, but she kind of knew where: here, in this bed – or one just like it – alone in the darkness, dropping endlessly into the emptiness, expired and expiring, dissolving back into the meaningless hotchpotch of chemicals that had made her. And all this hope and all this dreaming, just the strange twist of that particular cocktail that was her over-anxious, over-hopeful mind: and it would be gone too, passed into a noth-ingness from which another life would one day rise and one day fall, and rise and fall, and rise and fall, all this hoping and all this dying, rendered utterly useless when faced with the stark fragility and terrible quiddity of living.

She rises from her bed and goes over to the window. She stares into the blackness. Perhaps around the corners of the sky there are the first, faint beginnings of the day: tiny traces of dark ochre and purple are penetrating the gloom.

She drapes a shawl around her shoulders, puts on her sandals, and, picking up some jars of ointment from the table, steps into the night.

The second sound we hear: her footsteps on the path. Resolute. Determined. She will do what she promised: the one thing left to her – anoint his body properly for its burial. And remembering the way she had been mocked and reprimanded when she had poured oil from the same jar on to his feet, she shudders. Why had they always got it so wrong?

Now the day really is approaching. It is the blackest hour – the one before the dawn – but also the brightest, for even in the darkness, day is stirring. The light is winding its way around the world, waiting to break in to her small part of it. And other sounds accompany her: somewhere a dog is barking; a rooster screams at the impending day; everywhere birds are beginning to cackle and chirp, marking out their territory, doing what it seemed for a moment all created things must do: stake their claim, post their sentries, build their walls. She can even smell the morning. The tang of thyme and wild garlic hang in the air beside the paths she hurries down. And if anyone was to see her (though no one is around, it is far too early) they would imagine she was late for an appointment. She has about her the air of someone in a hurry. But deep within her it is very different. She is propelled by resignation. She has a date with duty, and all it recalls is all that is lost, and the signs of the approaching day are just a ghastly reminder that everything is the same as it was yesterday, the whole world circling ever closer to its own demise.

Her pace slows. She is now outside the town, nearly at the garden, nearly at the place where they laid him. All sorts of other practical questions fill her mind: will the soldiers let her through (they had placed a guard at the tomb, fearful that someone might steal the body away)? Will they help her move the stone so that she can go in?

She pauses at the entrance. Her heart is beating quickly. Almost there. This one last thing to do. Almost over.

But of course something has happened. Its noise will resound around the world, delighting and dividing. But at this vital moment there is nothing at all, not even a whisper. Something is happening, but it is not heard. That is the logic-shredding awfulness of it. Unwitnessed . . . you see he was that still, small voice, that unlikely and surprising presence of God. But not opened. Not yet.

And even if you'd been there, as she was there, there would have been nothing to hear. A moment out of time broke into time and there were no reverberations, nothing that we could measure or record.

Oh, there would have been noise. That's the strange thing. One thing does impinge upon another. But there was nothing to hear. Not yet.

In the moment of opening there was only darkness and silence.

And she rushes into the garden, suddenly sensing the awfulness of it, unaware, unknowing. And in a moment she beholds it. The guards gone. The stone rolled away. The tomb abandoned.

She stares in horror. It is hideously apparent what has happened, his body seized by some over-confident band of stupid zealots. It is also deeply frightening. There will be more controversy. More scandal. The temperature will rise again. This time it might consume her. Would it ever be over?

She looks to left and right, searching for any traces of where he might be or who might be close. But she is completely alone, and all she can see is a desecration. A cold fear, even more dreadful than the fears of the night, grips her heart. Even the opportunity for a last kindness has been stolen. And in that second an overwhelming despair rises within her. There really is no meaning left.

Somewhere deep in the heart of the universe a pebble falls into water. It is so far down and so far gone, you could not hear it, but its ripples fan out, little waves, vibrations in the air and in the seas, enough to move mountains.

Chapter 2

Why are you weeping?

Then there is terrible confusion. First of all she runs. Back along the paths from whence she came. Her feet pound the gravel. Her breath is sharp and laden. But she soon finds them – Peter and John – they are half awake, sprawled outside the house staring into the middle distance, seemingly oblivious that night has turned to day. They are neither awake nor asleep. They have about them that same pallor of weary resignation that she was wearing.

They see her approaching, but say nothing. She comes right up to them but it is as if she doesn't exist; they neither acknowledge nor dismiss her. And she is so out of breath that at first she can't speak. She stands before them, bending in pain, panting, breathless. Then the words just tumble out: 'They have taken the Lord out of the tomb.'

The words themselves drop like a stone. At first they say nothing, do nothing. They just stare at her, only now aware of her presence. And she wants to grab hold of them and shake them into action. They have both been so useless: one so patient, watching but doing nothing; one so active, but failing to watch and doing everything except anything that would do any good. So she says it again: 'They have taken the Lord out of the tomb. I don't know where they've laid him!' And something about the panic in her voice – the fear – alerts them. They look at each other. They seem to read each other's minds, and, without saying a word, rise up.

More footsteps on the path. Peter and John running. Running towards the tomb. But John is faster, and, outrunning his friend, he gets there first. He stands in front of the tomb. It is as she said. Empty. The stone rolled away. The body of Jesus gone. He bends down to peer inside. He can see the linen shroud lying there, but he doesn't go in.

Now Peter arrives. He pushes past him. He goes right inside. He also sees the linen wrappings. He sees the cloth that had been used to wrap Jesus' head rolled up in a place by itself away from the shroud. Everything is neat and tidy. It doesn't make sense. It looks neither ransacked nor abandoned. It has just been left. Not for the first time, it all seems beyond him.

But now John goes in. He crouches inside the tomb and looks carefully at the place where the body had been laid. He remembers all that he had seen on that bloody Friday afternoon. He remembers leaning on the Lord's shoulder at supper the night before. In his heart he still thinks of him as 'the Lord'. He has not let go of his hope. In his mind's eye he sees the bread breaking, sees it offered, shared, and then at the same time nails being driven in, blood spilling. For a moment it all comes together in his mind: 'This is my body broken for you. This is my blood shed for you. Do this to remember me.'

He catches hold of a thread which leads from this emptiness to that cup's fullness, and the Lord's determination to drink it and then at the same time to pour it out for all. And he can't explain it, won't yet proclaim it, nor even does he really understand it himself, but it is there inside him: suddenly a conviction, an understanding. He stands in the empty tomb. He sees and he believes. But he says nothing.

Then it is quiet again. The two of them step outside and she is waiting. Waiting to see what they'll say, waiting to see what they do. But again, nothing. Again, they hardly acknowledge her. They just trudge home, leaving her behind.

And now it rises within her again, and her tears flow unabated, unashamed. And as her body shakes with sobbing she remembers how he had delighted and confounded her, and how his words had been so rich with joy – always making her smile or weep – and always so hopeful. Even when it came to death, he had spoken of seeds waiting silently in the ground.

Through her tears she also bends to look into the tomb. To her amazement she sees two figures in white sitting where his body had been, one at the head and the other at the feet. Are they angels? She is startled. She shakes her head in disbelief. She doesn't know what is happening, but they look at her with a cool equilibrium. 'Woman, why are you weeping?' they say to her.

It is the most stupid, futile question she has ever heard, and she wants to scream at them. Isn't it obvious? Isn't it already painful enough? He is gone. He is defeated. He is humiliated. And now this! Not even permitted the rest of death. His grave plundered. His body snatched. And she pleads with them, not knowing who they are, not even caring where they have come from: 'They have taken away my Lord . . .' But her own words convict her: who is 'they', and why and how? The questions rise in her mind. The awfulness of it swells. 'I don't know where they've laid him,' she says to them, stating the obvious. And realizing that her own questions are as stupid as theirs, she stares up into the sky, up to the hills that surround Jerusalem. 'From whence cometh my help,' she says to herself, coldly, despairingly.

She is fixed to the spot. She cannot turn from the tomb, but she can't bear to look at it either. But there is no stillness inside her. She is agitated, disconsolate. The tears still flow down her face.

From somewhere behind her she senses the slightest movement of another person. She looks around, but still doesn't actually turn.

There is someone standing there. A man. A gardener?

She wonders how long he has been there. He seems to be looking at her, watching her. She suddenly feels embarrassed, and she is about to say something herself when he speaks: the same words as the angels, but this time they are beautiful, for there is a deep kindness in his voice. 'Woman, why are you weeping?' he says. And even as he asks, it is as if he knows; as if he can see and feel the pain that grips her, that holds her to this spot while the others have departed: as if she is still hoping to catch hold of a part of him whom she has lost.

She is weeping for everything that might have been, and for everything that was. Her body is wracked with the all-too-human pain of knowing that the precious beauty of living is wafer thin and easily broken; needle-in-a-haystack-small and easily lost; a pinprick of dazzling light in a dark and brooding universe and easily extinguished. And when you know this, and especially when its succour is drained by the inevitable deprivations of death and sadness, what can you do but weep and rage against the dying of the light? No, do not go gentle into that good night as he had done. What good was it? You were still dead. And she wanted to say all this. She wanted to scream it out and batter her fists against the awful emptiness of life, against this man appearing from nowhere and presuming to care: and yet the gentle tenor of his voice seemed to suggest that he already knew, that he was somehow with her in the mausoleum of her grief. Not just beside her.

Chapter 3

————————

Who are you looking for?

The two of them stand in the garden. The sun is just beginning to cast the fullness of its first rays across the dew-drenched earth.

She is standing in front of the tomb. Her body is still, but deep unrest convulses her spirit. Tears smudge her face. The stone that was placed at the entrance is pushed away to one side. He is standing beside her. Close to her, but not quite next to her. She is sort of half-turned round, looking at him, wondering who he is and where he came from. They can see each other clearly and they look at each other closely, but she is not turning round to face him properly. She has no idea who he is. And yet she has this strange desire to reach out to him. It seems as if he might know something.

She sees but doesn't see. She hears but doesn't hear. Like many before her, like so many after, she doesn't get it. Not yet. He is standing before her – the very one whom she is looking for – but she doesn't know it is him. Perhaps the early morning sun is in her eyes? Perhaps her tears have blurred her vision? Or is it something else?

'Who are you looking for?' he says.

Such a question. And she didn't know there was any more feeling to be dredged from the pit of her heart. But this question burns like fire. There is so much she is looking for, but in these last few weeks it had all focused itself into one person – into him – the one whose lifeless corpse she was seeking, the one she didn't know she was looking for until she found him, although even then it seemed as though he had always been looking for her. That was how it was for everyone who found him – who was found by him – his words and his presence seemed to chime with the deepest longings of the heart, not taking away all the other questions, but re-framing them within the knowledge of a great love, and the astonishing relief of receiving affirmation. To be loved and accepted; that was what no one else had ever given her in life – not without condition – and she didn't even know how much she wanted it (how badly she needed it) until it was found. Found in him.

'Who are you looking for?' She wanted to cry out: 'I am looking for the one who saved me. Isn't it obvious? The one who taught me how to be myself. Who accepted me. Who gave meaning back to me. Who put a spring in my stride. Who showed me other ways of living, and who taught me joy beyond possession, and who rid my world of fear.'

She had followed him. From the first moment she had heard of him to the day when she encountered him, to his un-equivocal acceptance of her, and his protection when others had scoffed and scorned. She had sought him out. She stood behind him in the house of that self-satisfied Pharisee and she had wept.

How strange! She had wept then as she was weeping now. And as her tears had fallen she had knelt at his feet and bathed them with her tears and dried them with her hair. Then she had kissed his feet and, breaking open the jar of ointment she had brought with her, she had anointed his feet. She shuddered with the memory. Those feet she had held, skewered to a cross.

Now when the Pharisee who had invited him saw this, he was full of righteous indignation. What is it about the religious, she thought, that they are so quick to judge? They take such delight in it. He puffed himself up. He was a proper, 'pleased with himself' man of God, knowing all there was to be known about the failings of others. He knew the location of every splinter. 'If this man were a prophet,' he said, looking around himself proudly, anticipating the applause, milking it, 'he would know what kind of woman this is who is touching him.' And she remembered his pointing finger, his condescending tone, his lascivious eye. If he could not touch her himself, he would make damn sure that anyone else who did was contaminated in his place. And it wasn't as if she had never experienced this before. No one was ever neutral about those in her trade. But it was worse in the presence of this accepting man, whose feet she held, because he had been pleased to receive her service – that was all – and this condemnation sullied him.

But he was never a weak man. And always impeccably mannered, always sure. He spoke back. 'May I say something to you?' he asked.

Another of his strange stories – a riddle: a certain creditor with two debtors, one owing 500 denarii, the other 50. Neither can pay. Both debts are cancelled.

'Which one will love him more?' he asks, nonchalantly, almost innocently. And the faintest whisper of a smile chances across his face. He leads them to condemn themselves. That was part of the mystery of his goodness. He never condemned anyone himself, just kept on pointing out the truth of things, till you either saw it yourself – God so loved the world – or crushed him in your rage. Which is, in the end, what they did. The logic of unfailing charity was always going to be too much to bear for those who had spent a lifetime avoiding it.

'I suppose the one for whom he cancelled the greater debt,' came back the reply.

And then he did smile. Not rudely. Not grinning. But an actual smile that even here recognition might dawn, hearts could be changed. That was what he was always after. He wanted to save them all. 'You have judged rightly,' he said.

And then he had turned to her: 'Do you see this woman? I entered your house; you gave me no water for my feet, but she has bathed my feet with her hair. You gave me no kiss, but from the time I came in she has not stopped kissing my feet.

You did not anoint my head with oil, but she has anointed my feet with ointment. Therefore, I tell you, her sins, which were many, have been forgiven; hence she has shown great love. But the one to whom little is forgiven, loves little.'

Then he looked at her very closely, so lovingly: 'Your sins are forgiven,' he said.

That was the beginning of it. The new life. This knowledge of forgiveness; this chance to start again, to be the person you thought you couldn't be: it was a revolution. And everyone else murmuring, reaching for their black caps: 'Who can forgive sins?' they mumble. Or what else could this money be spent on? What a waste, this costly oil. How grand to be so sure of yourself that you need no forgiveness, never need to look for anyone beyond yourself.

And now she looks again at the man beside her. It seems that he may know something. Who is he? Where did he come from?

She thinks to herself that he must be the gardener. Perhaps he has seen what has happened; perhaps he has moved the body himself. And she so longs to see that body one more time, to wash those feet again, to gently caress those wounds where the nails had been driven into him.

She had looked for him before and she had found him. She would look again. She would go on looking. She would do what she came to do.

21

She grips the jar of oil that she is still holding. There is new resolve in her: 'Sir,' she blurts out, 'if you have carried him away, tell me where you have laid him.'

Chapter 4

Mary

What's in a name? Well, as she was about to discover, every-thing actually.

He says to her, 'Who are you looking for?' And she replies in hope and exasperation, 'Sir, if you have taken him away, please tell me where.'

There is a moment's pause. The warmth of the sun is over-coming the coolness of the early morning air. The mist is dispersing. We are standing on the edge of a moment that will change human history. The whole world will be baffled and enchanted by this conversation; seek to discover what it means and where it leads. Every knee must bow before it. But first it has to be received: not as an explanation, or the triumphant flourish of a trump card, but as an invitation, the chance to inhabit a different world.

He holds her in his gaze. He looks at her with great tender-ness. He says her name: 'Mary.'

And as she hears her name, it is like a shot of adrenalin pumped straight into her vein and now she is focused, alive and alert as she has never been alive and alert before. All her anxious restlessness ebbs away. She is wide awake. She is turned around: literally swivelled and re-focused. It happens in an instant. A moment of release and a most glorious moment of capture. She turns from the tomb where she has been anchored, glued to the grief and horror of all her loss, and she turns to him: quickly, resolutely, like iron filings to a magnet, like a flower turning its face towards the warmth of the sun. It is Jesus. She knows it instantly. And yes, a rose by any other name would be as sweet, but her name, spoken by him, is a healing. It is a reawakening.

Everything changes. A whole new world is born. It is brought to life by the uttering of a name. A word of recognition in a world bruised and broken by anonymity, random violence and hurtfulness: all the things that had crushed her and all the things that, in the end, had crushed him. Only they hadn't! Somehow he had triumphed. Somehow love goes on. Jesus speaks her name, and joy – the joy of knowing and being known, of recognizing and being recognized – is planted in her heart again. That which was lost upon that cross and buried in that tomb is born again deep within her. She realizes it straight away, in the very unfolding of this moment: this man is a gardener – not the hired hand sweeping up the leaves in the municipal cemetery, but a new Adam, the one who will bring order and fruitfulness to God's creation.

The sun can now be clearly seen. Its round, reassuring luminescence sits on the horizon. Everything is lit up.

In the rest of Jerusalem the city is stirring. People are getting up and beginning to go about their daily lives. The Passover festival has ended. Things get back to normal. And she stands in the garden and realizes that nothing can ever be normal again, that everything has changed.

She is known and loved. It is a miracle to her. It is, I suppose, what all of us want. This is how she saw it: it was her daily reality – the people who knew her didn't love her. And those who loved her didn't know her. But putting the two together? That always seemed beyond her: an impossible dream, a miracle that she had never even dared hope for until she met him. He had changed the rules. What was it he had said to that other hapless woman, caught in the very act of adultery, about to be crushed by the mob: 'Let those who are without sin cast the first stone.' He stood up to them: defiant, unyielding, but never brutal or arrogant; just the assurance that sustained him, that there was another way of living, another way of inhabiting this earth. He showed that it could be a place where justice and mercy embraced. And while they fidgeted in their anger, he sat down and drew pictures in the sand, and one by one they drifted away. Because that is the point; she realized it now – none of us have clean hands. We are all compromised and soiled by our wrong choices. We all need the reassurance that we are loved, even when we are fully known. We all need forgiving, but we don't know where to find it. We all need the chance to start again, but have stopped believing it is possible. I am what I've become and I can no longer be what I desire. So when the crowds had departed he stood up and said to that woman, 'Where are they? Has no one condemned you?' And she said, 'No one, sir.' And he replied, 'Neither do I condemn you. Go your way, and from now on do not sin again.'

And that was what he said to the very men who strung him up on that cross: 'I don't condemn you.' That was what he was doing. He was living it out in himself – and especially in his dying – this refusal to condemn. He didn't want anyone to be lost. He didn't want anyone to be so consumed by their own hatefulness that they would miss the forgiveness he was offering. But the more you hate, the more you see the world from your own perspective; the more blind you are to everyone else, the harder it is to recognize. Was that what had blinded her for a moment?

She wipes the tears from her eyes. She recognizes him. Her face breaks into a smile, the smile of recognition. Things click into place. A great peace is secured in her heart.

Yet at the same time, as she thinks about it, she is baffled: she recognizes him now, so how did she fail to recognize him before?

You see, there is continuity and discontinuity. The one who stands before her is the same man who was fixed to the cross: tortured, humiliated, beaten and killed. Of this she has no doubt. It is Jesus. She apprehends this the moment he speaks her name. And yet, at the same time, he is not the same.

But he is not a ghost. His presence to her is physical, tangible, touchable.

He is present to her with a different sort of life. At some deep level she comprehends this instantly, although she would never quite know how to describe it, still less explain it. Only this: one moment he was with her and she didn't know who it was; and then the next – when he spoke her name – she recognized him.

But here is the deepest mystery: Mary Magdalene is looking at the first piece in the jigsaw of a new creation – not a corpse brought back to life, but the first piece of a non-corruptible physicality. It is as if a piece of the future is brought into the present: a living signpost.

That is the outward reality – not an absurd contradiction of the rules of nature, but the sign and starting point of a new creation. The stone that was rejected is now the cornerstone of a new building, a new Jerusalem.

But she isn't thinking any of this. It's just there inside her, to be puzzled over, debated, disagreed with for ever. For her, in that 'moment out of time come into time', it is love that propels her. For here he is, her beloved, the one whom she is seeking, standing before her in the brightness of a new day, and with the wide expanse of eternity before him.

He speaks her name – 'Mary' – and her eyes are opened, her ears unblocked. Like Adam giving names to all the creatures, she is named. And with the gift of a name the gift of a place, the gift of belonging. As she hears her name, she receives the gift, and at last she turns away from the emptiness of the tomb and all its hopelessness, and towards the one who is her hope. In the wilderness of her grief, flowers blossom and bloom.

'Rabbouni!' she says, which means 'Teacher'. It denotes respect. He was always their teacher, the one who instructed them. But it is also a friendly word of recognition, the name she would have used many times before as she travelled with him on the road. And as she says this word, she throws her arms around him. She wants to hold on to him and never let him go. He is alive!

Chapter 5

⇒•◦•⇐

Do not cling to me

When Mary says 'Rabbouni!' it speaks of continuity: the man standing before her is the one whom she saw crucified. When so many others had fled, she had stayed. She had even waited at the tomb that morning when Peter and John had drifted home. She wept and waited at the cross. She wept and waited at the tomb. Now those tears and that waiting are rewarded. So she holds on to the one who was lost to her.

But what is she holding?

The risen body of Jesus is not a resuscitated corpse, not someone like Lazarus, destined to die again. Jesus is alive with a new and different sort of life. It proceeds from what has gone before, but is also radically different.

Jesus wept at the tomb of Lazarus. He cried out, greatly disturbed in his spirit and deeply moved. So even the authorities who were watching him – always watching him, willing him to fail, urging him to falter – said of him, 'See how he loved him!'

He stood there, facing down death, and he ordered them to take away the stone. And when Martha, Lazarus' sister, tried to stop him, he rebuked her, saying, 'Did I not tell you that if you believed, you would see the glory of God?'

So they took away the stone. And he looked upward and said, 'Father', and now she remembered the strangeness of that, and also the comfort – calling God 'Father' – 'I thank you for hearing me. I knew that you always hear me, but I have said this for the sake of the crowd standing here, so that they may believe that you sent me.' And as she thought this, holding him, alone in the garden, she wondered with a rush of sudden anxiety: how will people know? How will people believe me, when there is no one else here to see?

Standing before the tomb of Lazarus, he had cried out so that everyone could hear, with a voice like thunder: 'Lazarus, come out!' But who will hear this?

He is alive with a different sort of life. She realizes it now. She can feel it in him. Lazarus rose from his tomb, still stinking of death's decay and struggling with the grave-cloths that bound him. But here was Jesus rising with the dawn of a fresh, clear day. The grave-cloths that bound him are neatly folded. Left behind.

Lazarus rose to die again. Jesus is raised with the new life of eternity and the promise of the new creation.

Then she remembered what he said: 'I am the resurrection.' Just those first two words were shocking enough: to say 'I am', to take upon yourself that sacred verb, the words that were themselves the perplexing heart of the mysterious name of the active and ever-present God revealed to Moses. But that other word: 'resurrection'. It is something different. 'Those who believe in me, even though they die, will live, and everyone who lives and believes in me will never die.' And then he had added, looking around at anyone and everyone, issuing an invitation to all: 'Do you believe this?'

And so she held him. Held him in the first flush of the new dawn of resurrection life; and she believed. How could she do anything else? But what she was holding and what she was believing were also a profound mystery. All she knew was that she believed in *him*. He had shown her another way of living, and he had come back from death and was standing with her. So what could be more natural than to hold on? With joy, she wraps her arms around him. The one who was lost is found. And she isn't going to let him go again.

But there is always more to learn. And even as she is thinking this, he is gently untangling her. Not violently, not a rejection, but carefully and lovingly unwinding her arms from around his waist.

There is continuity and there is discontinuity.

Mary is clinging to the Jesus she knew in his earthly ministry. But she is also holding that first piece of the incorruptible new creation. It has been formed out of the death of the old.

It is the same Jesus: but the seed that lay dead and buried in the ground is now risen with a new life that cannot be clung to in the same way.

This does not mean he is a ghost. What she holds is still matter. (Later Thomas will be invited to touch and hold this same risen body that Mary is told to relinquish.) It is a sign of two things: first, the newness of the life that is continuous with the old, but now incorruptible; and again an inner meaning: one that speaks across the ages to all who have life sewn up – do not think you can define or constrain me. Every time I am buried I will rise. Every time I am defined I will shake myself free, and you will be led – kicking and screaming if necessary – into new definitions and new understandings. But they will never be enough. There will always be more. For to know Jesus is to know God. 'To have seen me is to have seen the Father' – that was what Jesus had said on the night before he died. And to know God is to plumb the very depths of the infinite love, and of the very verb 'to be', through which the world was made and in which your own life is held.

Do you think this strange? Even when you do not fully know yourself? Even when you glimpse the untold potential of your own living? Even when you are endlessly finding new things in yourself? New things in the people around you and especially in the ones you love the best? Or when you glimpse again your deepest desires for yourself and dream again of the person you can be and not just the person you have become?

Love grows. It grows and multiplies. It receives and draws more strength. It is the same for ever, and it is born anew each day. Therefore this new life will also mean a new presence, and an endless leading into new truth. And as soon as you start thinking you have got it worked out, God will rise up. 'I am the resurrection,' says Jesus. And even for Mary, beyond this presence here, in this garden now, there will be a new and unconstrained availability: the promise of the Spirit. Of course there will always be temptation: a temptation to cling, a temptation to hold. We will doggedly hang on to all those comforting experiences of where God was for us in the past. But where is he today? Where is he now? Even as you try to hold him, he evades your grasp; he is dancing ahead of you with new challenges and new delights. 'He is not here. He is risen.' That will always be the strange message of Easter.

Chapter 6

My God and your God

In the same moment of her holding, there is also a releasing. He receives her and he lets her go, liberates her to be herself. 'Go to my brothers,' he says to her, 'tell them I am ascending to my Father and your Father, to my God and your God.' He propels her into the world.

More footsteps pounding the path. She is running again, and there is joy and purpose in her stride. God's future has broken into the present. She finds the disciples where we all must stand, crossing frontiers and on the edge of dramatic discovery, and blurts out the astonishing message of the first Easter Day: 'I have seen the Lord.'

They stare at her in dumb disbelief. They are on the same edge of that new creation where she was minutes earlier. A place where we all must stand, weighing the evidence, hearing the story, deciding how to respond. For there are other explanations: stolen bodies, wishful thinking, mass hallucination or plain deception. But those who cross over into this new land on this first Easter Day will take this story to the ends of the world. Will die for it. Is this a price you'd pay for a deception? Or is the wildest explanation the only one that makes true sense of what happens next? That he is risen; that there is new life.

So that is where they are standing when Mary stumbles into the resigned hopelessness of their situation. They have to decide.

Her story tumbles out; all that has happened, all that he has said. They keep on staring, their eyes wide open, their faces puzzled and perplexed. She says that he had seen her sorrow. That he had acknowledged her searching. That he had spoken her name.

These are such treasures. To be met at the point of the most crushing sadness. To find your heart's desire. To be known by name. Out it all comes. In a jumble of emotion and passion. And she can't tell whether they believe her or not.

Some turn away. One or two start interrupting with questions or complaints. Some scoff. But she is steadfast. 'I have seen the Lord,' she says again. That is the plain, brute fact of it, and none of their demanding proof or clarity, or any amount of 'Why her?' can change it. She waited by the tomb. She saw someone. She thought it was the gardener. He spoke her name and she suddenly realized it was him. That was what had happened. She was there in the darkness and she saw the light. She couldn't say more, but she wouldn't say less either.

And he had asked her to come and tell them. That was what she was doing, she said to them proudly and defiantly.

Mary is the first witness – the first person to tell this good news. That is how it will become known – good news for all the world.

She is the apostle to the apostles. And for those who still question the truth of this story, consider this: would anyone making up such a story choose a woman like this to be its central witness?

No, it is Jesus who commissions her. He meets her in her grief and points her back to life and to the proclamation that will form the mission of his Church. For this is all that Christian people have ever had to tell: 'He is risen.' And Christian life begins when we receive for ourselves the astonishing truth of this claim. This is our story: on the first day of the week, very early in the morning, while it was still dark, Mary Magdalene went to the tomb. And she saw the stone rolled away; and lingering there when Peter and John had left, she saw the Lord. And though she held him, and though it was good to feel him near, he commissioned her to tell others. And that is what she did. She told them what she saw. And they told others. And others, hearing that story, had their own lives changed, and they passed the story on, down through the ages, crossing the generations, century after century, person after person, one at a time, receiving and telling this astonishing story, trying to work out what it meant; whole communities formed by its telling, propelled, by its power, over and over, right down to this moment: my sitting here telling this story, trying to tell it in a way that might make us stop, and, hearing it as if for the first time, receive it afresh, know its transforming power, share it with others.

Go and tell. 'I am ascending to the Father,' says Jesus. That is also why you cannot hold on to me. My presence with you will be different now. But your destiny with me is assured. But note this: the Father of Jesus is now their Father as well. His God is their God. A new community is born. It is born out of the impact of the resurrection and the telling of the story.

PART TWO

LATE AFTERNOON

Chapter 7

⎯⎯➤•◀⎯⎯

What are you discussing as you walk along?

More footsteps.

Cleopas and his friend are leaving Jerusalem. They are in a hurry. It is late afternoon and the worst of the afternoon's heat is just beginning to subside. The sun is beginning its descent.

They are talking. Nineteen to the dozen. All about what has happened. As they leave the city walls behind, they look around themselves, furtively, as if they think they might be followed.

They head west, following the course of the sun. They are making for a village called Emmaus, where they plan to stop for the night. It will take them a couple of hours.

They seem dejected and agitated.

They talk about the prophet Jesus: the one from Nazareth; the one who has caused such a stir in the city; the one who was squeezed – the Roman authorities on one side, and his own religious leaders on the other.

They turn the events over in their heads. They try to make sense of what has happened; try to come to terms with their own feelings of loss and abandonment. For they too had been followers of this Jesus; not part of his inner band, but part of that larger crowd of people who had been drawn to him as his ministry of preaching and healing had meandered across Palestine.

They had heard him speak, and his words had power and clarity: they spoke directly to the heart, but at the same time made sense of everything else. So they had become two more of the many, many people who found themselves part of that strange travelling entourage of dreamers and schemers who were with him – some dreaming of revolution, others of heaven.

For them, it was just to be with him. There was something about him – especially his words – which were magnetic. Once you had heard them; once they had penetrated beneath the skin, underneath the radar of pride, there was no turning back. They were hooked. But not in a bad way. It was a liberation, not an addiction. His words had life. It was bliss to hear him speaking, to listen to the things he said.

But now he was dead. He had been executed. Brutally. Horribly. But, like so many of his followers, they had not actually witnessed this. It had all become too dangerous. They had made for the shadows. They thought they might all be rounded up.

They had heard the story. Everyone had. He had been betrayed by one of his own followers; convicted by some kangaroo court of the Pharisees meeting in the dead of night; taken before the Roman Governor; turned on by the crowd; stripped; beaten; crucified: chewed up and spat out – that is how it had seemed to Cleopas and his friend.

It had all happened with astonishing speed. And they were left reeling.

So they walk and talk. And everything that had seemed so full of hope was now plunged into grief and despair. And those big players like Peter and James, who had promised so much and who seemed so reliable, so wise: they disintegrated, they abandoned him too. And in the end he died alone – well, almost alone: John and Mary and some of the other women, they had been there. That's what they'd been told. But what good did it do? They couldn't stop it.

But neither could he. That was the painful point of it all. They thought he could. They thought that even then – standing before Pilate, or defying the cruelty of the cross – he might do something or say something that would make everyone see. But he didn't. As they hauled him up before Pilate he was virtually silent.

That was when many of them had stopped believing. For in the end it was hideous, violent, random. They trapped him. They stretched him out. They pulled him apart. It was all too easy for them. And at the last, he had nothing to say. His life was snuffed out, forgotten. And it was obvious to all of them that he was not a Messiah. Messiahs don't get crucified.

For that was the other reason they followed; it was the thing that united them all. They had started believing. One by one the belief had spread. Whispered at first, and then, in this last week, shouted from the rooftops – a real gauntlet thrown down to the compromisers and the lily-livered. They had started believing he was the Messiah, the one promised by God, the one who would set them all free. But it seemed stupid saying that now, in the light of all this.

They had got it wrong. That was the plain truth of it. But when they were with him, when they listened to him speak – then it had all been different. And although none of them could really agree on what they wanted a Messiah to be, even that faded away when he spoke, or even when you were just in his presence.

But he was not a Messiah. A good man? Yes. A powerful preacher, a healer, even? Yes. But not from God in the way they hoped.

So it was ended, and all that remained was confusion and regret. Their eyes were closed to him.

Over and over they went. Chewing at the bones of all that had happened. Picking the carcass. Looking at it from every angle. And always finding the same despair and humiliation.

They felt lost. They didn't know where life was going now they couldn't follow him. They felt stupid. They had placed such trust in him, such hope. And they'd been wrong.

Still half-a-dozen miles to walk.

Jerusalem is behind them.

It is clear what is happening now. They are getting out, leaving it behind. They are walking towards Emmaus: that much is factually true. But the deeper, harder truth is that they are walking away from Jerusalem. They are leaving all their hopes behind.

There is also an unspoken fear: what happened to Jesus might happen to them. The other disciples have locked themselves away. They are scared stiff about what might happen. They don't know which way to turn. There is no one to lead. They are all saving their own skin.

And something else nags away at them. There is disappointment that it has all gone so wrong. There is shame that they ended up getting it so wrong themselves. There is fear that they are going to be arrested, that there will be a price to pay. But there is also a whispering disturbance that it is not all quite over. All through the day, other crazy stories have been emerging. Normally you wouldn't pay them any attention, but the rumours were starting to spread like a virus. They were contaminated already. Peter and John had been to the tomb in the morning, and to their horror they had found the stone removed and the body gone. This was a real shock and no one seemed to know what had happened. Was it that the soldiers taken him away? But if so, why? Or had some of his own followers done it? But how? After all, there was a guard at the tomb. And were they going to say he had been raised from death?

Then someone had reminded them that he had said himself that if this Temple were destroyed he would raise it in three days. What did he mean by that? Was he speaking about himself? They shuddered at the thought.

Then some of the women – Mary especially, all worked up, defiant, adamant she was – said they had seen him. Seen him alive. This was the last straw. This was madness. And even though no one really believed her, of course some of them wanted to believe, and that was how the rumours started.

That was also when they realized they had to get out. Things were spiralling out of control, and these stories would only make matters worse. They would prolong the agony. Rile the authorities. They would all be rounded up. They would all be crushed.

So they stumble on. The path ahead of them is uneven. The shadows that fall behind them are imperceptibly lengthening. They turn the story over again. They try to make sense of it, justifying their own actions, looking for the clues that will enable them to wipe the whole slate clean, start again some-where else, somewhere away from Jerusalem and all its longings for God. For in that moment it seemed to them that there was no God, or that the God they had hoped in had never been real. Their eyes were closed. Closed to God. Closed to Jesus. Closed to hope. Nothing made sense any more.

Then – as if from nowhere – there is the steady tread of another pair of feet falling in beside them, picking up the rhythm of their steps. Another person. A stranger. They look at him, half startled that they never noticed his approach, but also glad of some company, someone who might take them out of themselves. They also wonder: how long had he been there? Had they been so caught up in their own conversation that they hadn't even seen him draw near?

He smiles at them, but they don't recognize him. It is true, the evening sun is in their eyes; but it is also true that they shield their eyes and look him up and down. But they don't know who it is.

For a moment no one says anything and a silence rests between them. There is no greeting, no introductions.

Then the stranger speaks. 'What are you discussing with each other as you walk along?' he says to them.

And this most innocent, most inviting of questions, has the effect of stopping them dead in their tracks. They look to the ground, downcast and subdued. As they think of what has happened it is almost as if there is no longer any point in going anywhere.

Cleopas replies: 'Are you the only stranger in Jerusalem who does not know the things that have taken place there in these days?'

The stranger smiles. 'What things?' he asks.

And then the story comes out again. Pouring out. More focused than before, but still as painful and as hopeless, as if you have dredged it so many times you get down to the one unavoidable kernel of the truth of it: 'The things about Jesus of Nazareth,' they said, 'who was a prophet mighty in deed and word before God and all the people, and how our chief priests and leaders handed him over to be condemned to death and crucified him. But we had hoped . . .' And as he said these words, he could hardly continue because this summed up the awful, hopeless pain of it all. Yes, we had hoped, and our hopes have been dashed. He pauses, catching his breath, resolving to go on. 'We had hoped that he was the one to redeem Israel. Yes, and besides all this, it is now the third day since these things took place. Moreover, some women of our group astounded us. They were at the tomb early this morning, and when they did not find his body there, they came back and told us they had indeed seen a vision of angels who said that he was alive. Some of those who were with us went to the tomb and found it just as the women had said; but they did not see him.'

Another silence. Their story finished. Another smile as the stranger hears and weighs all he has been told.

What are you discussing as you walk along?

Cleopas and his friend are unexpectedly unburdened. It has been good to tell their story to someone else, to get it out in the open. They even understand it better for telling it aloud. They see their own mistakes clearly. They had allowed themselves to be misled. They had followed a dream and it had spiralled into a nightmare.

And this stranger has listened with a gracious intensity. In a world of noise and distraction, where most people seem only to think of what they are going to say next, he has listened to their every word. His attention has never wavered. This in itself was a small healing.

And then he spoke again. 'You fools!' he smiled, 'So slow of heart to believe all that the prophets have declared.' Then, as they carry on walking, he starts to talk about the Scriptures. But he talks in a new way. He takes the old stories, but he sees them differently.

Chapter 8

———

Was it not necessary that the Messiah should suffer?

This is what he says. He begins with things long ago. He travels back into the very beginnings of their faith in order to plot a new course to the present. This is what he needs to show them; that what has happened was necessary, that it had always been this way, that the Messiah had to suffer these things before entering into his glory. It was what the prophets had foretold even if only a few of them had ever glimpsed what it might actually mean.

He started with Moses. He spoke about the night of the Exodus and the blood of the sacrificed lamb painted on the lintel of the doors and the angel of death passing over. He told how God had made a covenant with his people that night, but, like all the other covenants, we had failed to keep it. We had always gone our own way, hedged our bets, put our trust in ourselves, or hankered after the gods of prosperity and power that we found all around us. He said that even those who had been saved from death, liberated from slavery, the ones who had walked across the dry land of the Red Sea with walls of water to the left and right of them had, in the end, done their own thing and turned their back on God. And all the covenants, and all the rules and all the pleadings, did not change it.

He explained to them how all the prophets had spoken about this disobedience and this wilful turning from the way God had marked out, but it hadn't made any difference. Then one of them, Isaiah, had this vision of a servant, someone coming from God who would somehow suffer on behalf of all the people, someone who would carry their infirmities and would himself be wounded for their trans-gressions, crushed for their iniquities. And then he actually quoted the prophet: 'All we like sheep have gone astray; we have all turned our own way, and the LORD has laid on him the iniquities of us all.' For the prophet somehow saw that this servant of God would be oppressed and afflicted and would himself be like a lamb led to slaughter.

Then, speaking passionately, powerfully, drawing together the disparate threads of the tapestry of Scripture and creating a new picture, he went back further, back to the very first covenant God had made with our Father Abraham, and how God told him that he would be the father of a multitude of nations. He told of how Abraham's faith was tested. God had asked him to sacrifice his own son Isaac; and they went up the mountain, and Isaac said to his father, 'Father, we have kindled a fire to make this offering to God and we have a knife to make the sacrifice, but where is the lamb for the burnt offering?' And Abraham said, 'God will provide the lamb for the offering, my son.' And Abraham bound his son and actu-ally laid him on the wood and raised the knife to strike him. But at that moment an angel called from heaven telling him to spare the boy. Abraham looked around and saw a ram caught by its horns in a thicket. He took the ram and offered it instead. And we always thought that when Abraham said God will provide the lamb he was referring to that ram which he found when his faithfulness to God was proved true, but it wasn't. And neither does it just refer to the lambs that were slain on the night of the Exodus. And neither does it refer to the lambs that we slay year after year, Passover after Passover, because, in the end, the blood of lambs and bulls cannot take sins away, they are not pleasing to God. They don't work. No, it refers to something else. A new covenant that God was going to make. Something that would last for ever.

Don't you remember the prophet Amos raging against the futility of our sacrifices and our worship? He said: 'I hate and despise your festivals. I take no delight in your solemn assemblies . . . and even though you offer me your burnt offerings I will not accept them. Take away from me the noise of your songs; I will not listen to the melody of your harps. But let justice roll down like waters and righteousness like an everlasting stream.'

Or as it says in the psalm, 'Do I eat the flesh of bulls, or drink the blood of goats? Offer to God a sacrifice of thanksgiving, and pay your vows to the Most High.'

The prophet Micah put it very plainly, stating matter-of-factly what it is that God requires. Is it burnt offerings? Or thousands of rams? Or rivers of oil? Is it the sacrifice of a first-born for the atonement of your own sins? No, what God requires is this: 'To do justice, and to love kindness, and to walk humbly with your God.'

Here was the point. God and only God could provide the sacrifice, a life perfectly offered. The Lamb that God was going to provide was his son, not Abraham's. The Messiah had to suffer, because the Messiah was going to be that Lamb of God, that suffering servant. Not an earthly ruler, another David ushering in another human kingdom, but the one who would bring in the rule of God. That was the reason our people were marked out in the first place. It was so that the light of God might shine through them to everyone. But they always got it wrong. Either obscuring that light altogether, or just keeping it to themselves. The prophets tried to draw us back, but we would not listen. God had to enter the situation himself. Had to take the risk of being rejected, had to show us how to live. God, in the loving obedience of his son, had to be that Lamb of God that we could not offer and that we could not become. And at the same time, the Messiah had to suffer because we suffer. How could we ever know God's love if God was always beyond us? How could it be real if it was always the other side of all our suffering and dying? We needed a Messiah who was like us in every respect – one of us – and yet without the sinfulness that kept on meaning we got it wrong.

And so it was inevitable that such a Messiah would be rejected. That was what Isaiah saw, though even when he said it he could hardly have known what it meant. How could anyone? How could the Messiah himself? Because he too would come in the very likeness of the fragile flesh we inhabit, and therefore be subject to its constraints and demands, and especially its pains.

But he would be obedient. Even to death. He would live a life of perfect offering to God and perfect communion with God. He would, in this sense, carry the sins of the world. He would be the embodiment of God's people and live out perfectly that life of offering that we had failed to live.

At the same time he would show us the depths and the extent of God's love. He would, in that sense, be paying the price that none of us could pay. Because we couldn't live such a perfect life. We are always marred by our sinfulness.

Don't you remember Hosea saying that when Israel was a child I loved him? That I led him with bands of love, with cords of kindness like one who tenderly lifts a little child to his cheek. That is how God loves his people. That is how God loves his world. God will never give up on us. He will go on loving even if we never recognize him or accept him. There is nothing that can separate us from God's love.

But such a love can only be real if it is offered freely. That is what the Messiah does; the Messiah who suffers. And likewise, love can only be real if it is returned with the same freedom with which it is offered. God will not force himself upon you. God will not twist your arm. God will not play dice with you. He is steadfast, faithful, enduring.

What God always wanted was a relationship of love. God's covenant was always a marriage proposal, not a court order! So God does everything that is necessary to show the depth and nature of love. And then God waits. Waits for our response: the free response of our love to God's love. That was the reason the Messiah had to suffer. Not just because sins were forgiven, but because it was love.

Don't you remember what he said: 'When I am lifted up I will draw all people to myself'? That there is no greater love than this, that one should lay down one's life for one's friends? That is what he did. That was the reason he suffered.

Don't you remember all those stories? About lost coins, hidden treasure, even a lost sheep, for goodness' sake? It was always about love. A love that goes the second mile. A love that suffers to the end. That was the cup he drained to the dregs.

Cleopas and his friend listened intently. This stranger's words held conviction and precision. He knew the Scriptures so well. The things he said spoke to the heart of their malaise. For the humiliating death that Jesus had suffered just seemed to them to prove conclusively that they had got it wrong, that he wasn't the Messiah they had hoped for. But this stranger spoke about it differently. He said that Jesus was the Messiah they needed. That his death was a victory. That somehow love was at work upon that cross. That this was what God intended.

Their heads spun with it. No one had spoken about God like this before. Or had they? Their hearts burned within them.

Meanwhile the shadows of the day lengthened. They stretched back down the road, almost to Jerusalem itself. The sun burned a bright, deep orange as it sank beneath the horizon, casting its last bands of light across a sky that had begun its daily shift through the spectrum of colour from vivid red, to a deep, bruised purple and then to the sombre blackness of night. And as the light faded and the conversation continued and the questions bounced back and forth, they reached Emmaus. The time had gone so quickly, and even though it was nearly dark and they knew the day was ending, it seemed like the passing of a moment, that conversation on the road.

They stop outside the house where they are planning to spend the night. For the first time the stranger walks ahead of them. He is going on. But they urge him strongly: 'Stay with us. It is almost evening. The day will soon be over.'

So he goes in with them. He sits down with them. A table is prepared and he eats with them. But as the bread is brought to them, a shift takes place. The stranger, the guest, suddenly becomes the host. He takes the bread, slowly, purposefully. He holds it up as if he is inviting them to eat. He says the prayer of blessing; a prayer they all know well, a prayer of thanksgiving to the God who provides their every need, who watches over them and who feeds them.

And then he breaks the bread. It is again a moment out of time brought into time. And they are connected – all these moments, woven together, uniting. As he breaks the bread they see again another loaf on another night, broken and shared, and they remember words of dark foreboding – my body broken, my blood shed. And now they are mixed in with the words that the stranger spoke on the road about a God who suffers, about a death which was a triumph: a triumph of love and a demonstration of what love will do, that it will break for you, that it will shed its blood for you. Only . . .

And then, of course, he is a stranger no more. He breaks the bread, and they remember his words on the road, and their eyes are opened. Not just opened to this stranger's identity, but to the meaning, to the truth of who he is and what his death meant and where it led – not to a tomb, but to a table – here in their presence, suddenly made known to them in the breaking bread.

In the same moment he is gone. In that moment of recognition their eyes are opened and he disappears from their sight. And although they long to see him again, they also know they don't need to. Broken bread will be enough. It was sufficient for eyes to be opened. It will be sufficient until another day dawns, a day beyond the dawning of all the other days that will make up the slow, turning lifetime of a universe, the birth of a new creation, a new heaven and a new earth when they will sit at table again in a new kingdom.

And in that same moment – a moment which is an eternity, a moment that holds within it all that they ever need to know and will spend the rest of their lives unpacking – they get up and return to Jerusalem. They are propelled. They stumble and run and charge back along the same road. They are delirious with joy: the joy of a new beginning, of a new birth. It is night. But the light that is burning in their hearts illuminates their way and casts all fears aside.

They find the other disciples and the other companions gathered together. They tell what has happened. That he met them on the road. That he joined them at the point of their deepest desolation, when they had stopped believing and when everything seemed lost. That he had listened to them and walked with them even though they were getting out. That he had spoken to them words of clarity and truth that made them look again at all they thought they knew and see it in a new light: his light. That they didn't recognize him. Not then. But they had known him when he broke the bread.

Chapter 9

Peace be with you

What is peace? Is it the silence after the guns have finished firing? Is it the so-called security of knowing that my bombs are bigger and more powerful and more numerous than yours? Is it secured by guards and sentries? Must we always patrol our boundaries and build the walls higher? Will it only ever be a truce, a kind of half peace as we catch breath, pausing between volleys of fire? Must it always be defended? And must we always get our retaliation in first?

Or is there something else? Something beyond just a lull in hostilities? Can we ever dream of a day when swords become ploughshares and spears are turned to pruning hooks? Or will the brutal logic of the mutually assured destruction of fear always prevail?

And what happens to all that fear? It infects us. Suspicious eyes are turned on every stranger. No more might they conceal the risen Christ or, as at Mamre, veil the call of God. No one entertains angels any more. We turn our homes into bunkers. We install cameras. We bury our treasure deeper and build our walls higher. We prefer the shelter of captivity to the risky freedom of peace. For that is what it is. Now it dawns; even in the fast-approaching night, peace is trans-formation. It is the dismantling of barriers, the removal of barricades, the destruction of walls. Indeed, it is the endless building of bridges: from me to God and from God to every-one. Even a bridge into my own heart, casting fear and suspicion away. For this is revealed: he is a tombstone-rolling, barricade-busting God.

There is a shudder in the universe. As if something were awakening. Like pieces slotting into place, stones rolling away. Cleopas and his friend have hardly finished blurting out the same crazy tale that Mary had been spouting in the morning, and no one is quite sure what it means or whether to believe it, and suddenly he is there, standing among them, more walls ignored, appearing within the tomb of their own self-protec-tion. And he speaks of peace. He looks around the room at each of them. 'Peace be with you,' he says.

And they understand what he is saying just as instantly as they see him. It confronts them. They are startled. It is as frighten-ing as it is liberating. Something is beginning, and if it is good for them, it must also be offered to all. They know they are part of it. Not just part of its receiving, but part of its giving. It is peace for all the world: for those who are far off as well as those who are near. And this will be costly. It is a peace that is far beyond the half-kept treaties of the world. It is a peace that others will try to destroy, for it threatens their own power to exclude and control. A stone is rolled away and a rejected stone is now the centrepiece of a new building, a new city; and this sends tremors round the world, and in their wake the mighty tremble on their thrones. And because this new peace promises everything, it will require everything. The world must be reconfigured around it. The peace of Christ is reconciliation painfully embraced, a new beginning.

And each has to work out what it means for them, as we also have to work out what it means for us. For what is offered is the very peace that Jesus spoke about on the night before he died: a peace that the world cannot give, a legacy of love. And it starts where reconciliation must always start: with forgiveness.

Peter winces at the thought of it, remembering broken promises and suppressed dreams. Must he forgive and be forgiven so many times?

So of course they are frightened. They know they need to be forgiven. They also sense what they may be asked to do next.

They thought it was all over. It was only just beginning.

And in case you're thinking that only the one who has been wronged has the power to forgive, then now you know some more about why he had to suffer, why he had to become the smallest of all, why he had to be a victim. For only the victims of the most terrible outrages of sin and hate have the power to forgive. I can forgive the person who has wronged me, but I have no power to forgive the person who has wronged my neighbour. So that is what he did: he became the victim, the suffering one, bearing the sins of everyone, and carried on forgiving, carried on loving. So now he stands among them and is able to offer peace, forgiveness, the chance to start again, to put life back together differently. And that is why, in that instant, seeing him standing among them, fearing he was a ghost, but at the same time knowing that what was before them changed everything, they were afraid.

And he spoke to them again: 'Why are you frightened, and why do doubts arise in your hearts?' He spoke into their fear. He said things that cast fears away. His words were themselves a presence. They enfleshed him in the same way that he himself was the enfleshing of God's word. 'Look at my hands and my feet; see that it is me,' he said. 'Touch me and see; for a ghost does not have flesh and bones as you see that I have.' And when he had said this, he showed them his hands and his feet. So they looked upon the wounds of his suffering. They touched him. They held him. They saw the future, and at the same time found the present transformed. Now it was shot through with the stuff of eternity.

This was when fear turned to rejoicing; when they saw and touched the reality of it all. It was strange – knowing without knowing, understanding without understanding. But they could not deny what their eyes saw, what their hands touched. And this would remain. Even when the crowds bayed for their blood, when gallows were erected and debts collected. They could never go back from the truth of this moment.

He even asked for food. It was the evening of the first day of the new beginning: a new Exodus and a new Passover. It was the evening of the eternal day. And they gathered, and the Lord was in their midst, and they ate and drank. And that is what they would carry on doing until the table of their fellowship on earth became the banquet of heaven.

Chapter 10

As the Father sent me, so I am sending you

The last piece slots into place. The final turning of the lens. The evening of the first day draws to a close. Darkness falls. But its demons are cast out. Its fears vanquished. It can no more envelop the world. Its terrors are spent. 'Peace be with you,' he says again. And then words of dreadful, and at the same time joyful, intent: a commission; the beginning of the beginning; a story to be told to the ends of the earth; a story with a thousand parts to play: 'As the Father has sent me, so I send you.'

It was what they were half expecting. He always stretched them: not to breaking, to perfection. There was always a point.

But he never forced them. His command was also an invitation.

He helped them understand the Scriptures in a new way. The things he said opened their minds. It illuminated the path that was forming before them. 'The Messiah had to suffer and to rise from the dead on the third day; and repentance and forgiveness of sins is to be proclaimed in his name to all nations, beginning from Jerusalem.' They began to understand it.

Now the invitation. For here they were, the infant Church, in Jerusalem and yet at the same time in themselves a new Jerusalem. For he was a Temple. That is what God has established in his rising. Standing in their presence, a new place of worship and a new access to God. It was in him and through him that we can know God differently and live life differently. Their job was to tell the story. 'You are witnesses of these things,' he said.

This was their role: to speak and tell of all they had seen and heard. To tell a truth wrapped up in a story, to proclaim a message wrapped up in a person. And now it was inscribed on the stuff of their own lifetimes, so that the story and the message, and the person and the people, could never be separated. The invitation to others would never be to sign on a dotted line, but to enter the story, to join them around the table. And they would tell this story to anyone and everyone. They would take it to the ends of the earth and embody the transformation and forgiveness that it held. But standing there in that upper room, even though their fears were now replaced with joy, even though they could see it and believe it, they also knew it had to be taken to those who would never see as they saw, never touch as they touched. And it must have seemed impossible. How could they, a simple band of peasant fishermen, dreamers and misfits, a rudderless boat, steer such a course? How could such a story be written on their flesh in such a way that others could read and hear and hold?

And now there is another shuddering in the universe. Not an earthquake, nor a rolled-away stone, but the still, small voice of a whispered breath: 'Receive the Holy Spirit,' he says.

Then he breathes upon them. Breathes into them. The very breath of life itself, only it is a different life, his risen life.

It is upon them. It is within them. It is like a cleansing fire and at the same time an overflowing stream. It burns and refreshes. New truths are seared onto them. Reservoirs of compassion are poured into them. And that truth will always be apparent, even when they themselves get everything else wrong. And these living waters will always flow out of them, even when they themselves are feeling dry and parched. The things he said were now going to be said through them. There was a continuity. 'If you forgive anyone's sins, they are forgiven; if you retain anyone's sins, they are retained.' The authority that he had received from God he passed to them. From now on they would be his hands and feet and eyes and heart. It was as though they were his body and he their head.

The Church, which of course only means those who are gathered, was born out of the impact of his presence with them in that upper room. It was how it would always be born: people coming together, and from the dark depths of their searching and their aching, discovering the disturbing presence of his light. But it must always be sent. What they knew so well, standing there, being gathered and dispersed, is what we have forgotten. 'As the Father has loved me,' said Jesus, 'so I have loved you. Abide in my love.' There will always be a place for you here. 'As the Father has sent me, so I am sending you. You are my witnesses.' You tell the story of which you are a part so that others may find their place and be sent out in turn. Everyone must be gathered in, no fragment lost. Everyone must be sent out.

They sensed it stretching out before them, this great story they would tell and the many hearts that would be changed. His Spirit would do it in them. His words would be spoken through them. It would propel them further than they could ever imagine going, further than he had been able to go himself, for to this point his presence had, inevitably, been limited to them. But through them, by the impulse of the Spirit, it would be available to everyone. The sins of the world could be forgiven.

And even if this mission failed, even if no one ever responded, even if a thousand backs were turned, a million invitations to the banquet spurned, they would go on telling as he had gone on loving. The things he said demanded it. For his words were Spirit and they were life. And they stood there, bathed in the light of his presence, and breathing the fresh cool air of eternity.

Outside, it was night again. But the light they beheld dispelled the darkness. He was the radiant morning star. In him was life, and this life was the light of all people. A light that shines in the darkness. A light the darkness cannot overcome.

Peter also stood there with the others. He was a man who had got it wrong many times, a man who was keenly aware of his own need for forgiveness. He no longer imagined he could do anything very much by his own strength, and certainly not this. But with this Spirit in him he was also starting to breathe again, starting to dream again. But this time it was not about what he could achieve, nor about the plaudits he would receive: it was about what God could do within him, about how he could point to Jesus, and about God's words enfleshed in him, waiting on his lips, ready to do their work, unleashed into a barren world and slaking thirsty souls.

And he knew it wouldn't be easy. He was still the same person, prone to get it wrong, fearful of the cost. But there was resolve in him, a new determination. He remembered another time when he had also stood with the Lord. Like now, there had only been a few of them and the task ahead had seemed impossible. Many had left. They wanted the pyrotechnics of his signs, not the revolution of his words. 'Do you also wish to go away?' he had said to them. And somewhere deep inside him, Peter knew he did want to run, did want to flee, that he always longed for a simpler, more straightforward life, but at the same time there was no choice. What he had seen in Jesus could never be denied, and especially not now. It had changed him and there was no turning back: 'Lord, to whom can we go? You have the words of eternal life.'

Postscript

<hr>

A biblical note –
inhabiting the Scriptures

In writing this story of the first Easter Day I have tried imaginatively to inhabit the text of Scripture. One of the challenges with all Scripture is that those of us inside the Christian community know it so well that we often fail to be surprised by it. We bring to our reading too many assumptions. We find it hard to read it with that openness of mind that allows new layers of meaning or fresh insight to emerge. I hope that the imaginative approach to Scripture offered here will enable the reader to dwell in the story too, and to return to the text with fresh enthusiasm, ready to allow the text itself to speak afresh.

But this approach does not mean that we do not take proper account of biblical scholarship. The fruits of many centuries of reading the text are part of the interpretive dialogue. We are part of the ongoing life of the Christian Church in which a central activity is the reading and pondering of Scripture. Therefore everything we say about it rests not just on the text itself, but on the way our reading of the text has been shaped by the insights of others. But there is no need to labour the point. It is my hope that the fruits of such careful biblical exegesis are simply woven into the narrative of the book.

We also, inevitably, read it with the eyes of our own culture, and I am aware that at several points, and especially in the chapter where Jesus speaks to Cleopas on the Emmaus road, my reconstruction of that dialogue is heavily influenced by the questions of meaning that my own age brings to the text.

In the main I have tried to be faithful to the integrity of the different Gospel accounts I am following. Hence, with the exception of the first chapter, in Part One I have exclusively followed the account from John's Gospel and simply tried to occupy that story. It is a masterly narrative, and I feel I will have achieved more than enough if it simply encourages the reader to look at it again and to read it slowly. I have also not put words into Jesus' mouth. The words he speaks are the words recorded in Scripture. My intention is to enable us to hear them through the ears, experiences and questions of the other main characters in the story as they encounter the resurrection. Since the book is called *The Things He Said*, this seemed a sensible and important discipline. The story is constructed around these words and what they said to people then, and what they say to us now. The more I have reflected on these words, it seems to me that there are several other books waiting to be written which might construct a whole theology of presence and mission from these remark-able and surprising words.

As I say, the first chapter is an exception. I have imagined Mary Magdalene before daybreak. In doing this I am not just trying to prepare us for the shock of the story (it is so easy to forget that no one was expecting a resurrection) but also to capture something of the fear and amazement that is captured in the sparse abruptness of Mark's account. Hence the chapter has no title. It is the emptiness of a death and the coldness of a tomb that I want to express. And also the fact that the resurrection happens in darkness and in silence, un-beheld by anyone.

Part One of the book is told from the perspective of Mary Magdalene. Her place in the Gospel tradition is of crucial significance. She is the person who stands at the cross and the tomb. She is witness to the whole story. However, in Chapter 3 I have taken the liberty of going with one part of the ancient tradition which associated Mary Magdalene with the sinful woman we read about in Luke 7.36–50, who bathes Jesus' feet with her tears and wipes them with her hair, and then, kissing his feet, anoints them with oil. Of course this woman is never named. Apart from her presence at the cross in Matthew's, Mark's and John's Gospels, and her central place in the resurrection narratives in all four Gospels and especially John, the only other time Mary Magdalene is actually named is at Luke 8.2 where we are told about a woman: 'Mary, called Magdalene, from whom seven demons had gone out'. So we do not know the identity of the mysterious woman in Luke's account who bathes Jesus' feet (although in John's Gospel, Mary, the sister of Martha and Lazarus, is named as the one who anoints Jesus with perfume and wipes his feet with her hair). But Pope Gregory the Great gives us the first recorded example of her being named as Mary Magdalene, and from that point on, the tradition that this unnamed prostitute was Mary Magdalene gained widespread acceptance. I thought it should be acknowledged here that I am making use of this tradition. It helps emphasize a crucial point, not only about the generosity of God's love, but the way in which the resurrection story is entrusted to the most unlikely custodians. But there are also dangers. There have been times when the Church seems to have divided all of womanhood into either virgins or whores. I don't want to do anything to encourage this crude and unhelpful analysis. But we are told that Mary was healed by Jesus. We can, I think, legitimately conclude that her life was marked by gratitude and indebtedness to him. It is this, and her tenacious commitment to being with him in his death and in his burial, that make her such a considerable person in the story.

In Part Two, the late afternoon and evening, we stay almost exclusively with Luke, picking up the story of Easter Day, with Cleopas and his companion heading for Emmaus. However, in Chapter 8, I do slightly depart from my rule of only using the words of Jesus that are recorded in Scripture. It feels like a terrible audacity, but, without quite mustering the courage to put it in speech marks, what I have done is reconstruct the speech that Jesus might have made to Cleopas and his friend when it says, 'beginning with Moses . . . he interpreted to them the things about himself in all the scriptures' (Luke 24.27).

More able biblical scholars than me will have done a much better job than this. And of course what probably happened on the Emmaus road was much more of a dialogue than a speech. But the text does in a way invite us to make such a reconstruction, so I hope it is not a distraction but more of an invitation for further theological and imaginative scriptural enquiry. It was hugely enjoyable to write. The Old Testament Scriptures I have been drawn to are ones that seem to me to reveal the meaning behind the necessity of the Messiah to suffer, and, I hope, present this doctrine in a way that is accessible and relevant to the sort of theological questions we are asking today. In other words, it is a small example of how an Emmaus road-type dialogue continues. For we are still in a position today where the 'sent-out Church' needs to encounter those who are lost and searching and allow their questions to interact with Scripture.

When these two return to Jerusalem to share their story with the other disciples, there are close parallels between the Lucan and Johannine narratives. In both accounts Jesus appears to his disciples again and says, 'Peace be with you.' In both accounts he shows them his hands and his side and tells them that they are to be his witnesses. So at this point I have allowed myself to place Jesus' words in John – 'As the Father sent me, so I send you' – into what is essentially the Lucan account. Of course, in Luke, Jesus tells them to wait in the city to receive power from on high. For Luke, the coming of the Spirit will be told in the second half of his story, the Acts of the Apostles. But in John, the gift of the Spirit – Pentecost – is intrinsically bound up with Easter Day itself and the presence of the risen Christ with his disciples whom he commissions to bear his message and receive his authority. These are differences that the Church has always puzzled over, and while it suits the liturgical year to separate these events, it seems to me to make much greater sense to see all this as part of the essential Easter experience. So the book finishes with these words of Jesus which empower and commission his Church.

Discussion questions

If this book is being used by groups during Lent then the following questions might be useful discussion starters. I am suggesting a way of reading the book and discussing it over five sessions.

Begin each session by asking these questions:

- What did you make of this chapter/s?
- What thoughts and feelings did it/they evoke for you?
- What questions do you bring to this session?

Allow for a time of silent reflection. Allow people to speak in turn (if they wish). Collect together the questions people bring.

Then follow the questions for each session, making sure you also deal with the questions people have raised themselves.

Finish by reading the passage from Scripture set for the session.

After Chapter 1

The resurrection happens in silence and darkness and is greeted with as much fear as joy.

In pairs or as a small group:

- What were the disciples thinking and feeling on the Saturday after Jesus had been crucified?
- Why were the women who first came to the tomb so filled with fear?

All together:

- Why is the world still so fearful of Jesus?

Read Mark 16.1–8

After Chapter 3

Allow Jesus' first words to Mary Magdalene to sink into your own mind.

In pairs or as a small group:

- Why are you weeping? Who are you looking for?
- How does Christ knowing and sharing our sadness make a difference?
- What is it about Christ that we find so attractive?

All together:

- What is the world looking for? What does it need?

Read John 20.1–15

After Chapter 6

Jesus knows us by name and tells us that his God is our God. But he also tells us not to cling to him.

In pairs or as a small group:

- What difference does it make to our faith to be known by name and to know that the God and Father of Jesus is our God and Father too?
- What do we cling to? And how can we learn to let go?

All together:

- What would the Church look like if we stopped clinging to the ways we have known Jesus in the past and looked for him where he is now?

Read John 20.16–18

After Chapter 8

Jesus meets Cleopas and his companion on the Emmaus road and listens to their questions. He then opens the Scriptures to them and shows them what it meant for the Messiah to suffer and die.

In pairs or as a small group:

- What are the questions and stumbling-blocks to faith that we carry through life and that we observe in others?
- Does a suffering Messiah make a difference, and why?

All together:

- How can the Church listen to the concerns and questions of the world?
- How would the Church need to change if it were to enable the world to hear the questions of the risen Christ?

Read Luke 24.13–35

After Chapter 10

The gift of the resurrection is peace. The challenge of the resurrection is to live it and share it.

In pairs or as a small group:

- What is the peace the world cannot know?

All together:

- How can we share in the sent-out apostolic life of Christ?
- What would a sent-out Church look like?

Read John 20.19–23